ENDOR

We Christians know that we ought to pray as commanded to in Luke 8 by our Lord and Saviour, Jesus Christ. But how do we pray effectively to receive answers to our prayers? This is a great challenge, indeed. Personally, I have been challenged by this book. It is one of the only books that I have ever read that gives clear guidance on how one ought to pray in accordance with the scriptures.

This book is both informative in that it helps one to understand prayer. I believe that anyone who has been praying tirelessly without receiving breakthrough, needs to read this book in order to receive guidance on how to pray.

As Christians, we need to remember that in every circumstance that God came to rescue His people, it was as a result of prayer. This book by Dr Steve will guide you to pray the right way such that you may see God's wonders in your life.

By Pastor Bamuza Shirinda, Senior Pastor, The Resurrected Jesus Christ Church, Phalaborwa, South Africa.

Clear mental action, right thinking, an enlightened understanding, and safe reasoning powers, are some of the benefits of praying.

The Bible tells us that, Daniel knelt three times a day in prayer, Daniel 6: 9-10. Solomon knelt in prayer at the dedication of the temple 1Kings 8: 54-57. Our Lord in Gethsemane prostrated himself in that memorable season of praying just before his betrayal. Luke 22: 44-45.

Tim Downs asks, "Is it hard to pray to an unseen, infinite, omniscient being? You bet!". Living in this world so bathed in materialism, and prosperity gospel, sometimes you get the impression that prayer is a grocery list: "Our Father, who art in heaven... Give me, give, me! Seems to be the modern approach. This book could not have come at a better time than this!

I am privileged to know Pastor Steve, and to know that his intention, is for the salvation of his readers. This book, Effective Prayer That Brings Results is sent forth in this spirit to use for the quiet hour, vigilant meditation for the many who wish to seek and find treasures of God.

Wanja Kibera, PhD Clinical Psychology

EFFECTIVE PRAYERS

That will bring Results

Rev Dr Steve M Mutua

EFFECTIVE PRAYERS

Publisher

Stean Media Publishing
www.steanmediapublishing.com

First Edition

ISBN-13: 978-1-9163630-0-7 - E-book
ISBN-13: 978-1-9163630-1-4 - Paperback

Printed in the United Kingdom and the United States of America

Unless otherwise stated, all scripture quotes are taken from the
New King James Version*; with emphasis added or paraphrased.*

Publishing Consultants

Vike Springs Publishing Ltd.
www.vikesprings.com

For further information or to contact Rev Dr Steve M Mutua please send an email to: admin@steanmediapublishing.com

Rev Dr Steve's books are available at special discounts when purchased in bulk for church groups or as donations for educational, inspirational and training purposes.

Limited Liability

This publication is designed to provide accurate and authoritative information in regard to the subject matter covered. It is sold with the understanding that the publisher and author are not engaged in rendering physiological, financial, legal or other licensed services. The publisher and the author make no representations or warranties with respect to the completeness of the contents of this work. If expert assistance or counselling is needed, the services of a specific professional should be sought. Neither the publisher nor the author shall be liable for damages arising here from. The fact that an organization or website is referred to in this work as a citation and/or a potential source of further information does not mean that the author or the publisher endorses the information that the organization or website may provide or recommendations it may make, nor does the cited organization endorse affiliation of any sort to this publication. Also, readers should be aware that due to the ever-changing information from the web, Internet websites and URLs listed in this work may have changed or been removed. All trademarks or names referenced in this book are the property of their respective owners, and the publisher and author are not associated with any product or vendor mentioned.

DEDICATION

I dedicate this book to my wife, my dear best friend and life companion – Pastor Anna. Though I may have no words to express my appreciation for you, Anna, I do know that when God blessed me with you, He gave me the very best. Your unconditional love, commitment, enthusiastic spirit and passion towards the JCM ministry have brought it where it is and made me who I am today. Anna, I cherish your devotion to prayer and your personal zeal for the things of God. I love you, Anna. My life has been blessed through you. To my children Jeff, Jake and Jessie – you flood my life with an unsearchable joy, and it is a great reward to be your father. I love you greatly. To my daughter Delia, your cooperation in our family has been such a blessing to which we give God all the glory for.

To my spiritual sons, daughters and to the entire JCM Fellowship: your tremendous love and support are sacrifices I embrace with all my heart. I am committed to serving you in the Lord and love you all very much. Remember that, this is our time, this is our season and we shall become whom God has called us to be. Our greatest day begins today and many more lay ahead – I love you all!

ACKNOWLEDGEMENTS

Every achievement is strengthened by the cooperative efforts and sincere encouragements and I would like to take this opportunity to express my gratitude to these parties.

To my Heavenly Father, giver of life – thank You. Thank You for entrusting me with the responsibility to effectively deliver Your Message to many souls through this book.

To JCM Pastors, ministers, sons, daughters, strategic partners, friends of the ministry, Luton Community and JCM precious congregants: your support and belief in me has inspired me to hold on to prayer. To this, I say thank you!

To Minister Oyin – your contribution towards this book was enormous. Thank you for being a great encourager, burden carrier and help to proofread the book. I want to say thank you.

Special thanks to my parents, Mum and Dad and also to my spiritual parents Bishop Dr Charles Marita and our entire family. May the Lord God almighty richly bless you.

I also thank my publisher Victor Kwegyir of Vike Springs Publishing Ltd. for the intellectual and technical support to piece this work together. God bless you.

May you encounter the favour of our Lord and Saviour as you read this book and choose to change your prayer life forever.

MAY GOD BLESS YOU ALL!

TABLE OF CONTENTS

FOREWORD

It is an honour to call Rev. Dr Steve M. Mutua my spiritual son. It was with him that I shared great platforms with ministering in Kenya. He is a man of integrity and discipline and I am a witness of what God has been doing in his life.

I encourage you to read this book on prayer. Once you do, your life of prayer will never be the same again.

Bishop. Dr Charles Marita. Visionary Christian Revival Church. Nakuru, Kenya.

The believer is unlike any other person on earth in the sense that he has a "cheat sheet" which is advantageous in any situation. This is because of the breath of the Almighty, which grants him with clarity of these present times. The Holy Spirit is God's own Spirit and we are scripturally taught that the Holy Spirit bears witness that we are sons of God. Isn't it amazing to be assured that you are approved as belonging to God? Sadly, some believers are oblivious to this truth and the devil brings in anxiety, depression and fear which prompts them to question their identity and sonship.

It is God's plan for us to stand strong in the face of trials and temptations. He wants us to put on His whole armor, through living a prayed up life, in order to stand in the face of adversity. This concept of effective prayer is exactly what this book seeks to explicate. By the end of this book, you will be able to comprehend the gravity of the scripture that instructs us to pray without ceasing such that it becomes a mantra. Prayer is not just mouthing off words offhandedly – it is strategic and must be effective. If you want to have a more effective prayer life, then this book is for you. It will teach you what limitations there are to prayer and how you can develop a consistent connection with God. Faith is highlighted in this book in that it stamps out any iota of fear through diligent studying of the scriptures and repeatedly hearing from God.

It is no doubt that this book is packed with nuggets to cultivate a lifestyle of effective prayers. It offers insight on how to get rid of the faith-distorting wiles of the devil such as offense and distractions in the form of thoughts etc. This book concludes with a call to engage the Anointing that is already upon you as a believer. The Anointing prepares you and equips you with all that is needed to fulfill your God given purpose.

By Pastor Victoria Oladipupo MA Theology and Religious Studies – Senior Pastor Freedom House London.

INTRODUCTION

It is one thing to teach prayer and another to actually pray, which is why we find that many teach prayer, but few intercede. What makes prayer unique is that it transcends beyond global cultures and traditions as many find themselves praying to a "god" and expecting sovereign intervention. Even Atheists, known as non-believers, go into prayer as a means of easing fear, anxiety and coping with life's challenges because prayer works! Since the Fall in the Garden of Eden, it is continuously being proven that human beings crave the existence of a Sovereign God. All great men and women of God in the Bible practised prayer. The practice of prayer is evident within the Christian, Islam, Jewish, Buddhist and Hindu community.

It was at the age of 17 that I walked away from religion and gave my life to Christ. Considering the type of people Jesus called, I realised that Jesus has no regard for our positions in this world. My witnessing of many miracles taking place through prayer were what ignited my passion for prayer. I have witnessed the blind see, the lame walk and lives being restored through prayer and through His Word. In my years of engaging in prayer, the

Lord led me to establish an overnight prayer force in Luton, which has been running for over ten years. My revelations brought through prayer have been collected in this book so as to ignite your passion for prayer. May the Lord empower you to engage in prayer until your marital situation, health, finance and career change positively in Jesus' name.

Writing this very book, I stumbled upon this precise scripture:

> *"As He prayed, the appearance of His face was altered, and His robe became white and glistening"* – Luke 9:29

If you are ready, this book then is for you.

CHAPTER 1

PREPARATION

> *"God has cast our confessed sins into the depths of the sea, and even put a, "No fishing", sign over the spot".*
> Dwight L Moody

*B*efore we approach God, we need to examine ourselves and ensure that our relationship with Him is right. Are you righteous or evil? A righteous person is he who has repented of his sins and accepted Jesus Christ as God's Son and his saviour and this is further reinforced in Romans 10:9. Is it not obvious, then, that an evil person is anyone who rejects Jesus Christ as Lord? God answers the prayers of the righteous, but the evil do not have that promise from Him. Therefore, do not be discouraged when your friends are not happy with the changes you are making in life owing to your newfound redemption. If the Lord is calling you to be born again, He is calling you to change your life and live for Jesus. He is inviting you to allow Him to work within you so that you can see His faithfulness, therefore do not look for anybody's approval. Only look for His approval and tell Him, "God, I am glad that you took me just as I am". The good news is that what you can't tell your spouse or pastor, you can talk to God about it because He is faithful. The moment you call upon His name, He will respond because He has been waiting for you.

In the Book of Peter, it is clearly illustrated that once we repent and become righteous, God is able to answer our prayers because His eyes and ears are upon us. Once you have God's ear, do not present your whole shopping list to Him. Rather allow Zion to take the lead; begin to worship and adore Him. God is a Sovereign Spirit and He created you to worship Him. You should therefore approach Him in humility and gratefulness, recognising His greatness and might. It is by worship that God moves on behalf of His children. This is again reinforced in James 5:16

"The prayer of a righteous man is powerful and effective". – James 5:16

"For the eyes of the Lord are on the righteous, and His ears are open to their prayers; But the face of the Lord is against those who do evil" – 1 Peter 3:12 (NKJV)

SUMMARY:

This book echoes the writings of the various authors used by God in the area of prayer. We will conclude this chapter by reiterating the following:

- ➢ God answers the prayers of the righteous.
- ➢ God does not despise a broken and a contrite spirit.
- ➢ You become righteous by believing in Jesus.
- ➢ Once cleansed, approach God with confidence.
- ➢ Approach Him giving reverence for who He is and enter His gates with worship.

CHAPTER 2

FAITH IS THE ASSURANCE AND CERTAINTY

"Weave in faith and God will find the thread"
– Unknown.

The Bible defines faith as the assurance of things hoped for. Faith is the vehicle that drives the answer to your prayers. Our faith is not in faith itself, but in God. I take steps in faith because I believe in God's character, He can never fail. As human beings, we always want assurance that the results we expect will be achieved. I will not go to Siberia if I am not sure that I am going to have warmth once I get there. Brethren, what is your faith in? There is more to faith than constantly asking. Hebrews teaches us that without faith, we cannot please God. As believers, we must also develop our faith to another level by realising that He who began the good work in us – the God we are praying to – is faithful to bring His work to a good accomplishment. He is the Author and Finisher of our faith.

> *"And without faith it is impossible to please God, because anyone who comes to Him must believe that He exists and that He rewards those who earnestly seek him"* – Hebrews 11:6-7.

Faith magnifies God's ability. Fear, which afflicts approximately 93% of believers, causes us to doubt God's ability. The Book of James tells us that a doubting person shall not receive anything from God. The enemy knows this and therefore attacks your mind with doubt

> *"Ask in faith without any doubting, for the one who doubt is like the surf of the sea, driven and tossed by the wind. For that man ought not to expect that he will receive anything from the Lord, being a*

double-minded man, unstable in all his ways" – James 1:6-8

How, then, does faith come? Romans 10 explains that faith comes by hearing the Word of God because you cannot have faith outside of God's Word. Thus, you need to know what Christ says and take Him by His Word, regardless of your situation. It is produced by God's Word, therefore anything outside of the Word is not faith. Interestingly, both faith and fear come by hearing. These are two contrasting phenomena and you cannot claim to have both. Faith is neither passion, nor is it a positive confession. The difference is who you hear from. Hearing from God brings faith and hearing from the devil brings fear. Hence, you should always pray by including scripture when you make requests to God. God says we should remind Him of His promises found in the Bible.

When you have faith, you begin to do what you were not able to do in the past. You receive an ability within yourself and you begin to realize that some of the things you struggled with before, you no longer struggle with them anymore. Some things that were a challenge to you, will no longer challenge you. Some situations that engulfed you causing you not to progress, will no longer be so anymore because that yoke of the enemy that was over your life has already been broken!

Child of God, it doesn't matter what you are going through or the situation you are in. Believe God; He that called you into ministry is the same faithful God that has made a promise over your life. Utilizing your faith, you need to make these declarations as you walk, declaring, "I know that the Anointing of God is upon my life. I am persuaded that through the good things He has started in my life, He is able to bring it into a good accomplishment in Jesus' name". Once it has been spoken over your life, it is always in your life. It is your responsibility to maintain it by studying the Word and holding onto those promises.

The thoughts others have about you do not matter, neither does the past that they hold in their custody. All that matters is your connection with the Lord and your proclamation by faith that what the Lord has called you to become is in your season and time. It shall come to fulfilment in Jesus' name. Declare with faith that you are aware of that Anointing upon your life. You are proclaiming the good news to the nations and testimonies of what the Lord has done for you in the name of Jesus. He is faithful and He is King over your life.

Stand on God's Word as you pray. Dare Him and remind Him of what He says. Develop an attitude of faith to draw God's attention to your situation. Even if things seem delayed, don't give up because faith in God always prevails to produce answers to prayer. And I can assure you, you will see it happen. Giants of faith are remembered because they hold onto God whether it happens or not. "I will hold on to His Word. If God said it, I believe it" – and that settles it. Most of Jesus' miracles were performed in response to people's faith. In Mathew 9:2, Jesus saw the paralysed man's faith and said, "Take heart, son; your sins are forgiven".

SUMMARY:

- ➢ Owing to our fleshly nature, we want assurance and certainty.
- ➢ Faith is assurance in God and fear is the opposite thereof.
- ➢ Doubt from Satan causes us not to receive from God.
- ➢ Faith comes through listening to the Word of God.
- ➢ Jesus healed many because their faith moved Him.

CHAPTER 3

CONFIDENCE IN GOD DEVELOPS PERSEVERANCE

"Faith is deliberate confidence in the character of God whose ways you may not understand at the time"
– Oswald Chambers

"Oh, how great peace and quietness would he possess who should cut off all vain anxiety and place all his confidence in God"
– Thomas A. Kempis

The practicality that faith gives us is confidence which God expects of us to be able to utilise in enduring and overcoming the challenges of life. Jesus Christ is the prime example of One who was crowned in confidence and the ability to endure. He endured the Crucifixion because of His assurance in His Eternal life which awaited Him. Endurance ensures that you remain on the right track of receiving results from God. When you are confident in Whom you have believed, then endurance falls into place. Confidence is attained by the Holy Spirit who empowers us. There is no need to pray if your confidence in God is wavering because faith without works is dead. Confidence in God will also make you do whatever He asks you to do. My faith in His ability emboldens me and helps me to stand on His promise.

> Hebrews 12:2 says, "Let *us fix our eyes on Jesus, the author and perfecter of our faith, who for the joy set before him endured the cross, scorning its shame, and sat down at the right hand of the throne of God*".

The times when we have to wait for the promises of God to come to pass are not easy times. At times our patience is tested to see if we still love Him. As a true follower of Jesus Christ, you must learn to love Him whether He provides for you or not. In Hebrews, the apostle teaches us not to cast away our confidence saying, *"Do not cast away your confidence, which has great reward. For you have need of endurance, so that after you have done the will of God, you may receive the promise"* – Hebrews 10:35. Hence, the devil attacks your confidence by throwing doubt at you. His aim is for you to curse God and walk away from your faith. But God expects us to endure. To endure is defined as the following: "to hold out against; sustain without yielding". I define endurance as holding on in integrity without compromising. In prayer, our faith builds confidence in God and because of that confidence, we are required to endure. We who are called by God's name must develop resistance to any situation. We need to realise that because our faith is worth more than gold, it will be put through fire a lot. Enduring in prayer and waiting on God without doubt is the firing process that refines the gold that you are. It was in prayer that the Lord revealed to me that endurance doesn't mean that the challenge is removed. It means that the Anointing of God in you, due to the confidence you have in Him, empowers you to endure the challenge. And in all this, I am confident that His grace upon your life will empower you to outlast any challenge.

1 Peter 1:6-8 reinforces this, saying:

> *"In this you greatly rejoice, though now for a little while you may have had to suffer grief in all kinds of trials. These have come so that your faith—of greater worth than gold, which perishes even though refined by fire —may be proved genuine and may result in praise, glory and honour when Jesus Christ is revealed. Though you have not seen Him, you love Him; and even though you do not see Him now, you believe in Him and are filled with an inexpressible and glorious joy".*

Peter is very straight forward here. When prayers seem unanswered it is because your faith is being tested so that it may be proven genuine and bring glory. Therefore, do not be discouraged in prayer; endure because God is all out to answer your prayer. Paul, a great man of prayer said, *"I am confident of this, that he who began the good work in you will carry it on to completion until the day of Christ, Jesus"* – Philippians *1:6.* It was my faith in God that enabled me drive 15 miles on an empty tank in June 2011. My faith in God empowered me to outlast the challenge, overriding the natural with the spiritual; this was a miracle. Miracles result from confident faith in God. Do not shake because your

God can be trusted; build your confidence in Him. Remember the Words of James: *"Be patient, then, brothers and sisters, until the Lord's coming. See how the farmer waits for the land to yield its valuable crop, patiently waiting for the autumn and spring rains. You too, be patient and stand firm, because the Lord's coming is near"* – James *5:7-8*. Be patient and wait for the answer to your prayer. It will manifest as long as it is prayed for according to your faith and it is in God's will.

SUMMARY:

➢ You must be confident in God.
➢ When the answer is delayed, your faith is being tested.
➢ Your confidence in God helps you to endure.

CHAPTER 4

PRAYING THE WORD – THE WILL OF GOD

> *"Prayer is an earthly licence for God's intervention"*
> – Dr Myles Munroe
>
> *"To know the will of God is the greatest knowledge, to find the will of God is the greatest discovery, and to do the will of God is the greatest achievement"* – Unknown

Anybody can pray and this is evident by the fact that billions of prayers are offered to God

17

per hour, if not per second. But the only prayer God hears, and answers is the prayer done according to His Word. God honours His Word, which is His law such that He created through His Word. He does not contradict what He has stated. In the beginning was His Word and He was the Word. He accords the same respect to His Word. David says in Psalms 138:2, *"You have magnified Your Word above all Your Name"*.

When you come to God due to bodily pain, you place it under His Word because it cannot be placed above His Word. You recognize that It is more powerful than your pain and that it has to give way to God's Word. Therefore, go around with the hurt assured that you are healed because God has said it. Christian singer, Ron Kenoly, echoing Isaiah 53, asked in one of his songs, "Whose report will you believe?", to which he responded, "We shall believe the report of the Lord".

> *"For the Word of God is living and powerful, and sharper than any two-edged sword, piercing even to the division of soul and spirit, and of joints and marrow, and is a discerner of the thoughts and intents of the heart"* – Hebrews 4:12.

God expects us to pray according to His Word and live according to the standard in His Word so as to position us to pray according to His written (Logos) and His revealed (Rhema) Word. The easiest way to receive a response from God in prayer is to pray with His Word. Before engaging in prayer, establish the will of God concerning the situation by studying His word. I believe that it is dangerous to ask for God's will to be done when it has not been revealed to you. What if what you desire is not His will? Or what He wills is not what you desire? In Isaiah, the will of God was for King Hezekiah to die. But Hezekiah, not wanting to die, faced the wall and prayed to live. God then added fifteen more years to his life, but those years were filled with many tribulations as it was not the initial will of God for him to live. You should, hence, seek God's will and align your prayer therewith. Fortunately, His will is revealed in the Bible. You need to pray with the scriptures and quote them to your circumstances because the Word of God is the power of God. When the Word is released to any situation, It's inherent power takes over and changes things. We pray in the name of Jesus and with the Word of God for effective prayer. A will, in terms of legal documentation, specifies how a person's wealth is to be distributed after their death. Jesus died and His will, God's promises in the Word, was distributed. You have a right to all the promises now as His dear child. God's promises are your inheritance so ask and they shall be given to you. He who tarries in God's presence, presenting scriptures to God, will surely win and prevail with God. God's Word is His covenant with the New Testament believer. Therefore, you ought to remind Him of His covenant by praying with His Word. Quote the scriptures to your sick wounds, combined with faith in His ability to heal. When you are overcome with fear, quote that even though you walk through the valley of the shadow of death, you will fear no evil. God Himself tells us that His Word is settled and cannot be changed, we can therefore depend on it. So, what are you waiting for? Begin to pray God's Word to Him!

In Hosea 4:6, God says, *"My people perish for lack of knowledge"*. To me, knowledge is the rightful application of God's Word in your situation. We perish when we don't pray in knowledge, that is, when we don't pray according to God's Word. God's Word and the name of Jesus is so powerful that demons tremble at their mention. Use the Word in spiritual warfare because it is the Sword of the Spirit. Pray with it and you will see God rise to honour His Word to answer your prayer. May the Lord empower you in faith that you may clothe yourself with the strength promised to help you rise up from the situations that have crowded your faith.

In Isaiah 55:10 – 12, God tells Isaiah about the efficacy of His Word, saying, "...*Instead of a thorn bush, will grow the juniper and instead of briers, the myrtles will grow*"

Once God's will for a particular situation is established, it is an act of disobedience and rebellion to pray for a different will because you are contradicting the authority of the Lord. The Lord does not contradict Himself and we therefore need to be doers of His will. Jesus desired to do the will of His Father. Since we are God's children, we too need to ensure we do His will so that our prayers are not hindered.

I would like us to agree in prayer.

> "Father, I pray for those searching your Word as you've allowed me to minister this Word to all that hear my voice, I pray that You, the King of Glory, may also minister unto them. I arrest every spirit of confusion in Jesus' name and I release the presence of God as we share the love of Christ. In Jesus' name, amen!

I believe that God has a great plan for you and that what He has intended to do with your life will manifest and bring the difference as you engage in prayer.

SUMMARY:

- ➢ God honours prayers offered according to His Word.
- ➢ His Word is His will.
- ➢ God's word is established forever.
- ➢ God's Word cannot go back to Him void.

CHAPTER 5

REALIZING THE SHIFTING OF ENTITLEMENT

"But as many as received Him, to them gave He power to become the sons of God, even to them that believe on His name" – John 1:12.

"For He has rescued us from the kingdom of darkness and transferred us into the Kingdom of His dear Son"
– Colossians 1:13

As a child of God, you are not a beggar, neither are you a liability to God! You are a son, His Child – beloved and precious. You have an inheritance in Him. As a child of God, you do not come to him pleading for scraps from under the table. According to the Word of God, Jesus responded to the Syrophoenician woman in Mark 7:28 clearly stating, *"Crumbs are foods for the dogs"*. All of God's children have access to eat from the table with Him. Therefore, your attitude in prayer should not resemble that of an unworthy servant, but of one who has a relationship with a loving Father.

I am reminded of my relationship with my daughter Jessie, she approaches me with total confidence. I am her Dad, and she asks expecting no opposition. She is my daughter and it is her natural inclination to ask from me believing that she will receive her request. She deserves it not because of anything she has done, but because she is my daughter and as a father, her voice is music to my ears; I want to hear it over and over again.

Equally, our Heavenly Father delights in hearing our prayers. The Father delights in answering the prayers of His children and He wants to hear you pray. Have it in the back of your mind that you are a child of God. Let your prayer stand on the sonship and the benefits which you are rightfully entitled to. It is a slap on His Person if you, His child, come to Him like a slave. In essence, you are doubting the power of the blood of Jesus that saved and qualified you as God's son.

Prior to being saved, we were estranged from God because we were not even fit enough to be His slaves – we were shameful through and through. But when we confessed Jesus Christ as Lord, God adopted us as His sons, and we gained the same rights as Jesus Christ. We, therefore, ought to approach Him the same way Jesus did. Apostle Paul instructed us to approach His Throne of mercy with boldness. Let us then fearlessly and confidently draw near to the Throne of God's unmerited favour to us sinners, that we may receive mercy for our failures and find grace to help in time of every need.

Pray with your head held up high and ask God expecting to receive an answer like a child would from a father. As a young Christian, I remember approaching God in prayer like an unworthy servant and not as one who has been accepted by Him and it is sad that some of God's children still approach the Father in the same way.

I believe we need to pause and reflect; how would you feel if your child came to you saying, 'Mummy or daddy, I know I am not worthy, but if you would, could you kindly buy me school shoes? I don't deserve the good ones; all I deserve is just anything to go to school with". You would not expect your child to approach you in such a depressing way, why then would you think God is pleased with you approaching Him like you are worthless?

Your entitlement to God changed the moment you believed in Jesus and was reconciled back to Him. Now you have the right and authority to decree something and it will be done for you. As it is said in Job 22:28, *"Thou shalt also decree a thing, and it shall be established unto thee: and the light shall shine upon thy ways"*.

As Jesus says, you should ask that you may receive. You can now seek with boldness, knowing that you will find. You can knock on "Daddy's" door knowing that it will swing open at the sound of your knock.

Peter and John exuded boldness at the Beautiful Gate when the lame man was being carried in. When he saw Peter and John about to enter, he asked them for some money. Peter and John looked at him intently, and Peter said, "Look at us!" The lame man looked at them eagerly, expecting some money. But Peter said, "I don't have any silver or gold for you. But I'll give you what I have. In the name of Jesus Christ, the Nazarene, get up and walk!". He jumped up, stood on his feet, and began to walk! Then, walking, leaping, and praising God, he went into the Temple with them. Peter and John made a decree in Jesus' name and the lame man was instantly healed! The testimony above does not read of two Apostles who were not sure of their place in God. We see Peter and John boldly asking for something to be done in Jesus' name. Do you think God reckons them more as sons than you? No, He does not. The scripture is clear; everyone that receives Him is given the power to become a son of God.

Given that you are righteous, answered prayer is your entitlement. "But when I sin, do I not lose my right as a son?" No! The prodigal son reconciled with his father, whom he had previously disappointed. In his dirt, his Father embraced him and ensured to clothe him with the best robe. Don't let sin bend your back. We all make mistakes and we all offend God. Once you realise where you have gone wrong, repent and ask God for forgiveness. You are never out of His love. When the enemy reminds you of your past, you should remind him of his future. You have been forgiven by God. When condemnation comes, stand on God's Word and remember that your past will not determine your future and that your future is in the hands of God. You are in Christ; you are not condemned. You are now justified. Your sins have been removed from you, never to be seen again. Approach God right now as His son or daughter. Pray to Him with boldness, fellowship with Him in confidence as He is a Father who loves you so much.

> *Therefore, there is now no condemnation for those who are in Christ Jesus* – Romans 8:1 (NIV).

> *And that as far as east is from west, that's how far God has removed our sin from us* – Psalms 103:12 (CEB).

SUMMARY:

➢ As a believer, you are God's Son. So, make your request to Him boldly, ask like a child loved by the Father.

➢ You ought to repent when you sin and accept the forgiveness of the Father to move on.

CHAPTER 6

Overcoming Barriers to Prayer

> *"No one is a firmer believer in the power of prayer than the devil; not that he practises it, but he suffers from it"*
> *–Guy H. King*

Prayer is the spiritual wavelength which we use to make our requests best known to God. Wavelength and prayer are not visible but have clearly visible results.

The enemy utilises many barriers to discourage you from accessing your Father in heaven, such as:

UNCONFESSED SINS

God does not understand the language of sin and hates it so much that He sent Adam and Eve out of the Garden of Eden when they sinned. If God could not condone the sin of the only two people on earth at the time, how much more the sin of billions? The devil distorts our minds so that we end up approaching God with unconfessed sins. Before engaging in prayer, ask the Holy Spirit to remind you of any unrepented sin and repent of each one as it becomes clear to you. Do not offer a prayer of "blanket forgiveness", such as, "Dear Lord, please forgive me of all my sins". Instead, be specific and render your heart in brokenness and sincerity. Beloved, remember that the devil has been here before the creation of man and has extensive spiritual and physical knowledge about human beings. One of the places that the enemy is always targeting to attack you through is your body. When Jesus said, "Destroy this temple and on the third day I will raise it up", He was referring to His body which the devil had been attempting to capitalise on to cause Him to sin against His Father. In doing so, the devil made statements that triggered Christ's flesh by asking Him to, "Change these stones to bread". Jesus, however, used the Word to resist the devil's temptation and he fled. Note that it was after Jesus resisted all the temptations of the devil that He returned to Galilee in the power of the Spirit.

Therefore, to overcome the flesh, we need to know the Word and receive help from the Holy Spirit to achieve the desired result, as explained in Acts 1:8 assuring us that we shall receive power when the Holy Spirit comes upon us. The good news is that Jesus Christ has already released the Holy Spirit for us, and we now have the Power of God and His Word. The Word of God energised by the Holy Spirit is both a manual and the weapon that we use in overcoming Satan. You must have knowledge of God's Word to effectively use it, as stated in Hosea 4:6.

DISTRACTIONS WHILST PRAYING

When you pray according to the Will of God, the devil is aware and may bring distractions to stop you from praying. He interferes using a variety of things such as a phone call or text, an unexpected visit or a reminder to complete a project. He may even place thoughts of what you should do after prayer. Note that he is not telling you to stop but cleverly engaging your mind with things other than prayer. If the resistance is too much to bear and you feel as though your prayers are not going beyond your ceiling, start praying in the Holy Spirit as He leads. The devil does not understand what you are saying, and you will feel energised to stay in God's presence longer.

OFFENCE

A great barrier to prayer is holding onto offense. Jesus says that if you bring a gift to God but remember that your brother has something against you, you should leave the gift at the altar and go make peace with your brother first. Though offence is inevitable, we should let go of it and forgive those who have offended us. We do not have the assurance of answered prayer if we hold offense in our heart and unforgiveness to our brother or sister. Realistically speaking, some offence is painful to let go of, but we must pray to God to help us release it and He will see our grieved heart and will heal us. As a minister of the gospel, I have experienced offence and being aware of its detrimental effects on one's spiritual and physical health, I have ensured to seek God fervently for a release as well as humbling myself to seek forgiveness from those that I have offended. I have also prayed with people who had been crushed by offence and irrespective of how this was brought about, the pain is excruciating. Therefore, do not be discouraged if you experience difficulties. Difficult times require us to have support from God-fearing people who have our best interest at heart. They also require us to obey God for the benefit of our soul.

Scholars have concluded that holding onto offense and negative feelings can manifest physically as illness. As a child of God, our bodies are the temple of the Holy Spirit and we have a responsibility to maintain a holy environment to propagate a healthy prayer life which results in a healthy lifestyle. We should, therefore, let go of offence.

As I sat to write this paragraph, I pondered on the many ministries, marriages, child and parents' relationships, business partnerships and friendships that would have been saved had the parties chosen to let go of offence. I am, thus, reminded of Apostle Peter in the Bible who when he asked Jesus how many times one should forgive a brother or sister, Jesus replied seventy times seven.

> "Then Peter came to Jesus and asked, "Lord, how many times shall I forgive my brother or sister who sins against me? Up to seven times, Jesus answered, "I tell you, not seven times, but seventy-seven times" Mathew 18:21-22.

Again, in the Book of Luke, Jesus spoke to His disciples in preparation of the ministry, advising them that offence is common and will surely come but it is our responsibility to forgive when it comes. "Then He said to the disciples, it is impossible that *no offenses should come, but woe to him* through whom they do come! It would be better for him if a millstone were hung around his neck, and he were thrown into the sea, than that he should offend one of these little ones. Take heed to yourselves. If your brother sins against you, rebuke him; and if he repents, forgive him. And if he sins against you seven times in a day, and seven times in a day returns to you, saying, 'I repent,' you shall forgive him. *And the apostles said to the Lord, "Increase our faith."* We see Apostle Peter applying this wisdom when he accepts forgiveness from the master. He also advises married couples to live in harmony with each other so as not to hinder each other's prayers.

> " *Likewise, husbands, live with your wives in an understanding way, showing honor to the woman as the weaker vessel, since they are heirs with you of the grace of life, so that your prayers may not be hindered"* 1Peter 3:7

Since our Lord confirmed that offence would surely come, it is our responsibility to ensure that we are equipped in the area of forgiveness so that our prayers are not hindered.

LACK OF FAITH:

In any relationship, trust is crucial as it forms the basis of our expectation from each other. In our relationship with Jesus, it is important to trust that He is the Able God that will solve every issue because He created the universe and placed us in it as His loving children. In the Bible, we note that when Jesus walked on earth, those who benefited from His miraculous works were those who expressed their belief in Him and then exercised their faith. Similarly, we note that Jesus did not perform miracles for those who were without faith. For our prayers to be answered, we need to have faith in God and exercise the instructions given in His word. For the Bible admonishes, "It is impossible to please God without faith. Anyone who wants to come to him must believe that God exists and that he rewards those who sincerely seek him" – Hebrews 11:6.

"A person who has doubts is like a wave that is blown by the wind and tossed by the sea. A person who has doubts shouldn't expect to receive anything from the Lord. A person who has doubts is thinking about two different things at the same time and can't make up his mind about anything" (James 1:5-8) Without faith it is impossible to please God; thus, faith is important to have answers to our prayers. Faith is built by studying God's word and is essential in

having our prayers answered. When we ask from God, we ought to believe, as the Word of God teaches us that, a man who doubts is like a wave which is constantly tossed around by the wind. He is unstable in his thinking and shall not receive or nor should he expect anything from God.

ASKING WITH THE WRONG MOTIVES:

It is important to examine the motive behind our asking because our prayers are offered to a Holy and loving Father who is just and sovereign and cannot be manipulated against His will for His children. In recent times, I have noticed a gap in the area where children of God pray seeking vengeance and retaliation against their brethren. When you pray to God with ulterior or selfish motives, do not expect God to answer your prayer. James' letter highlights that our prayers go unanswered because our requests are for our own pleasure and seek only to feed our human lusts. Therefore, we should ensure our motive is right when we pray.

When the answer to your prayer comes, will it be to God's glory? Overcome this barrier by abstaining from selfishness and consciously start thinking about how you can expand God's kingdom.

Let us explore a scenario that will help us gain a deeper insight into our Father's commitment to His children irrespective of the petition from Prophet Balaam who had been hired by an earthly King, Balak, to manipulate God against His children. We find that when love is lacking, all evil manifests.

Numbers 22:1-38

"Then the children of Israel moved, and camped in the plains of Moab on the side of the Jordan across from Jericho. [2] Now Balak the son of Zippor saw all that Israel had done to the Amorites. [3] And Moab was exceedingly afraid of the people because they were many, and Moab was sick with dread because of the children of Israel. [4] So Moab said to the elders of Midian, "Now this company will [a]lick up everything around us, as an ox licks up the grass of the field." And Balak the son of Zippor was king of the Moabites at that time. [5] Then he sent messengers to Balaam the son of Beor at Pethor, which is near [b]the River in the land of[c]the sons of his people, to call him, saying: "Look, a people has come from Egypt. See, they cover the face of the earth, and are settling next to me! [6] Therefore please come at once, curse this people for me, for they are too mighty for me. Perhaps I shall be able to defeat them and drive them out of

the land, for I know that he whom you bless is blessed, and he whom you curse is cursed."

[7] So the elders of Moab and the elders of Midian departed with the diviner's fee in their hand, and they came to Balaam and spoke to him the words of Balak. [8] And he said to them, "Lodge here tonight, and I will bring back word to you, as the Lord speaks to me." So the princess of Moab stayed with Balaam.

[9] Then God came to Balaam and said, "Who are these men with you?"

[10] So Balaam said to God, "Balak the son of Zippor, king of Moab, has sent to me, saying, [11] 'Look, a people has come out of Egypt, and they cover the face of the earth. Come now, curse them for me; perhaps I shall be able to overpower them and drive them out.' "[12] And God said to Balaam, "You shall not go with them; you shall not curse the people, for they are blessed."[13] So Balaam rose in the morning and said to the princes of Balak, "Go back to your land, for the LORD has refused to give me permission to go with you." [14] And the princes of Moab rose and went to Balak, and said, "Balaam refuses to come with us."

¹⁵ Then Balak again sent princes, more numerous and more [d]honourable than they. ¹⁶ And they came to Balaam and said to him, "Thus says Balak the son of Zippor: 'Please let nothing hinder you from coming to me; ¹⁷ for I will certainly honor you greatly, and I will do whatever you say to me. Therefore, please come, curse this people for me.' "

¹⁸ Then Balaam answered and said to the servants of Balak, "Though Balak were to give me his house full of silver and gold, I could not go beyond the word of the LORD my God, to do less or more. ¹⁹ Now therefore, please, you also stay here tonight, that I may know what more the LORD will say to me."

²⁰ And God came to Balaam at night and said to him, "If the men come to call you, rise and go with them; but only the word which I speak to you—that you shall do." ²¹ So Balaam rose in the morning, saddled his donkey, and went with the princes of Moab.

Balaam, the Donkey, and the Angel

²² Then God's anger was aroused because he went, and the Angel of the LORD took His stand in the way as an adversary against

him. And he was riding on his donkey, and his two servants were with him. ²³ *Now the donkey saw the Angel of the* Lord *standing in the way with His drawn sword in His hand, and the donkey turned aside out of the way and went into the field. So Balaam struck the donkey to turn her back onto the road.* ²⁴ *Then the Angel of the* Lord *stood in a narrow path between the vineyards, with a wall on this side and a wall on that side.* ²⁵ *And when the donkey saw the Angel of the* Lord, *she pushed herself against the wall and crushed Balaam's foot against the wall; so he struck her again.* ²⁶ *Then the Angel of the* Lord *went further, and stood in a narrow place where there was no way to turn either to the right hand or to the left.* ²⁷ *And when the donkey saw the Angel of the* Lord, *she lay down under Balaam; so Balaam's anger was aroused, and he struck the donkey with his staff.*

²⁸ *Then the* Lord *opened the mouth of the donkey, and she said to Balaam, "What have I done to you, that you have struck me these three times?"*

²⁹ And Balaam said to the donkey, "Because you have [e]abused me. I wish there were a sword in my hand, for now I would kill you!"

³⁰ So the donkey said to Balaam, "Am I not your donkey on which you have ridden, ever since I became yours, to this day? Was I ever [f]disposed to do this to you?"

And he said, "No."

³¹ Then the LORD opened Balaam's eyes, and he saw the Angel of the LORD standing in the way with His drawn sword in His hand; and he bowed his head and fell flat on his face. ³² And the Angel of the LORD said to him, "Why have you struck your donkey these three times? Behold, I have come out [g]to stand against you, because your way is perverse[h] before Me. ³³ The donkey saw Me and turned aside from Me these three times. If she had not turned aside from Me, surely I would also have killed you by now, and let her live."³⁴ And Balaam said to the Angel of the LORD, "I have sinned, for I did not know You stood in the way against me. Now therefore, if it [i] displeases You, I will turn back." ³⁵ Then the Angel of the LORD said to Balaam, "Go with the men, but only the word that I speak to

you, that you shall speak." So, Balaam went with the princes of Balak.

[36] Now when Balak heard that Balaam was coming, he went out to meet him at the city of Moab, which is on the border at the Arnon, the boundary of the territory. [37] Then Balak said to Balaam, "Did I not earnestly send to you, calling for you? Why did you not come to me? Am I not able to honor you?"

[38] And Balaam said to Balak, "Look, I have come to you! Now, have I any power at all to say anything? The word that God puts in my mouth, that I must speak."

SUMMARY:

➢ God is loving and just and cannot be manipulated to contradict His will.

➢ So, for our prayers to be answered, let us therefore ensure that our motives are clean and pure.

CHAPTER 7

Receiving from God

Man is created in the image of God and exists in trinity too:

God, the Father
God, the Son
God, the Holy Spirit

MAN IS

Body
Soul
Spirit

John 14:11-14 The Message (MSG)

"Believe me: I am in my Father and my Father is in me. If you can't believe that,

43

believe what you see—these works. The person who trusts me will not only do what I'm doing but even greater things, because I, on my way to the Father, am giving you the same work to do that I've been doing. You can count on it. From now on, whatever you request along the lines of who I am and what I am doing, I'll do it. That's how the Father will be seen for who he is in the Son. I mean it. Whatever you request in this way, I'll do."

After you have offered your prayers to God and you are waiting for an answer, the next thing is to believe by faith that you have been granted attention and the Holy Father has listened. For some of us, answers come immediately and at times, they come gradually. Through research, I have found that the majority of Christians do not know how to receive from God. The Lord revealed to me that He is a spirit and the delivery of our expectations happens at the spiritual exchange table. It is our responsibility to pull down the released blessings from the spiritual level to our physical being, as our blessings becomes most beneficial at this level. As long as our blessings remain on the spiritual realm, we will continue to struggle waiting. It is said in John 3:13: *"Beloved, I pray that you may prosper as your soul prospers"*. Once you pray and

God answers it, your desired blessing is released immediately. When my son asks me for a new pair of trainers, in my mind I have already provided it for him. I set money aside for it in my budget and then look for time to go to the shop to get it for him. Technically, he has it the moment he asks for it, but it will materialise when we take the action to visit the shop physically.

In Daniel Chapter 10, we read of how Daniel prayed, and God answered his prayer the same day, as the Bibles states, *"The very day you asked, I answered"*. Daniel waited for the physical manifestation which arrived on the 21st day of his fast. The lesson here is that God answered the moment Daniel prayed but it took time to physically manifest.

> A reminder from the Word, *"For everyone who asks receives;* those *who seeks finds; and* those who *knocks, the door will be opened. 'Which of you fathers, if your son asks for a fish, will give him a snake instead? Or if he asks for an egg, will give him a scorpion?"* – Luke 11:10-12

SUMMARY:

- ➢ God listens when we pray.
- ➢ Delays do not mean that you have been denied.

CHAPTER 8

Make A Decision

You can literally decide today and say, "Lord, I've heard about your ability to respond to my prayers. I have decided to change my life and choose to depend on you. Lord, I want to relinquish all my burdens and come to You just as I am. I accept the Lord Jesus as my personal Saviour. Now that I am born again, I surrender my life to God."

If you have made that prayer, you are now born again. Your name is written in the Lamb's Book of Life. If the rapture occurs today, you'll be mounted up in the sky with those that are also born again no matter how long you have been born again. From this day onwards, your victory, joy and success is assured. All you lay your hands onto will be victorious in Jesus' name!

Please reflect on these scriptures about your destiny as you continue to grow in Christ and develop a relationship with Him waiting for the soon return of our Lord Jesus Christ!

Revelation 13:8:

And all that dwell upon the earth shall worship him, whose names are not written in the book of life of the Lamb slain from the foundation of the world.

Revelation 20:12:

And I saw the dead, small and great, stand before God; and the books were opened: and another book was opened, which is [the book] of life: and the dead were judged out of those things which were written in the books, according to their works.

Revelation 3:5:

He that overcometh, the same shall be clothed in white raiment;and I will not blot out his name out of the book of life, but I will confess his name before my Father, and before his angels.

Revelation 21:27:

And there shall in no wise enter into it anything that defileth, neither [whatsoever] worketh abomination, or [maketh] a lie: but they which are written in the Lamb's book of life.

Revelation 20:15:

And whosoever was not found written in the book of life was cast into the lake of fire.

SUMMARY

➤ For any relationship to remain healthy communication is paramount.

➤ It is important to cultivate an environment that will ensure answered prayers.

➤ As the day of our LORD draws near, having a structured, dedicated prayer life will strengthen our faith till the day.

➤ I believe you are blessed and you will be a doer of His word.

God bless you.